My World
Your World

The Food We Eat

by Ellen Lawrence

Ruby Tuesday Books

Published in 2015 by Ruby Tuesday Books Ltd.

Copyright © 2015 Ruby Tuesday Books Ltd.

Editor: Mark J. Sachner
Designer: Emma Randall
Production: John Lingham

Photo credits:
Alamy: 4, 6 (top), 9, 10 (left), 16 (top), 17, 19 (left), 21, 22; Corbis: 8
(left), 19 (right), 22; FLPA: Cover, 2, 5, 12–13, 15, 22; Shutterstock:
5, 6 (bottom), 7, 8 (right), 10 (right), 11, 14 (left), 14 (right: Claudio
Zaccherini), 16 (bottom), 18, 20 (africa924), 22, 23.

Library of Congress Control Number: 2014958144

ISBN 978-1-910549-10-0

Printed and published in the United States of America

For further information including rights and permissions requests,
please contact our Customer Service Department at 877-337-8577.

**The picture on the front cover of this
book shows people enjoying a winter
cookout in Sweden.**

 Contents

Words shown in **bold** in the text are explained in the glossary.

All the places in this book are shown on the map on page 22.

What Foods Do We Eat?

It's porridge for breakfast in Namibia.

A school lunch of sausage and fries in Germany.

A delicious dinner of vegetables and noodles in the United States.

This family in Rwanda grows the vegetables they eat in their own garden.

Fruit is a popular food all over the world.

In Malaysia, many people eat durian fruit. The flesh of this fruit smells like strong cheese and onions, but it tastes like custard. In Mexico, people eat black sapote fruit. Its nickname, the chocolate pudding fruit, describes how it tastes!

Durian fruit

Black sapote fruit

A Very Important Food

There is one food that people eat all over the world—rice.

Rice is a type of grass plant.

The rice grains we eat are the plant's seeds.

People grow and eat more than 40,000 different types of rice!

Rice grains

Sweet treats made from puffed rice cereal

A farmer planting rice plants

Rice plants grow best in places where the land is very wet. Often farmers flood their rice fields with water from nearby rivers. In some places, farmers use water buffaloes to **plow** the wet, muddy fields before the rice is planted.

Farmers plowing the flooded fields with water buffaloes

Rice growing in flooded fields on a hillside in Vietnam

Delicious Bento Boxes

Imagine opening your lunchbox to see your favorite animal or cartoon character. In Japan, that's just what many children get to do every day.

The colorful lunchboxes are called bento boxes.

Japanese moms turn food into animal faces, superheroes, cars, flowers, and many other shapes.

A bento box

The main food in a bento box is usually rice balls. The **ingredients** used to make the meal might also include seaweed, mini hot dogs, salmon, omelettes or hard-boiled eggs, cubes of cheese, **pickled** vegetables, and fruit.

A teddy bear face made from a rice ball, sliced hot dog, and seaweed

9

Sweets for Diwali

The **festival** of Diwali is celebrated by Hindu, Sikh, and Jain people around the world. Diwali is also known as the festival of lights.

Diwali celebrates the victory of light over darkness and of good over evil.

It is also a time of new beginnings.

An oil lamp

Giving friends a sweet will make them think sweet thoughts of you.

People set off fireworks and decorate their homes with small oil lamps.

Everyone eats lots of homemade sweets and gives boxes of sweets as gifts.

The Diwali sweets in this picture are from India. They are made from many ingredients, including flour, beans, lentils, carrots, pumpkins, nuts, raisins, and yogurt. Sweet **spices** such as cinnamon and nutmeg are also used.

Food from a Forest

The Baka are a group of people who live in **rain forests** in Africa. The Baka are **hunter-gatherers**. They hunt or find their food in the forest.

Baka men use spears and arrows to hunt for antelopes, crocodiles, and monkeys.

Women and children catch fish, turtles, termites, caterpillars, and giant land snails to eat.

A giant land snail

Baka people find mushrooms and fruit such as berries in the forest. They also search for beehives in trees. Then they gather the honey to eat.

This Baka boy is licking honey from some honeycomb.

13

Food from Yaks

Many people around the world get most of the food they eat from their animals. In Tibet, people raise hairy cattle called yaks.

Yak farmers get meat and milk from their yaks.

Patties of yak dung drying in the sun

Yak butter for sale in a market

People also collect yak dung, or poop.

Then they dry the dung and burn it as fuel for cooking and heating.

Tibetan people make butter from yak milk. The butter is mixed with water, tea, and salt to make butter tea. This warming, fatty tea is the favorite drink of people in Tibet.

A yak pulling a sled loaded with hay to feed the yak herd

15

Fish and Chips

In the United Kingdom, many people love to eat fish and chips. It's **traditional** to have this food for supper on a Friday night.

Most towns in the UK have a fish and chips shop.

On Friday nights, there are often long lines of people waiting to buy their food.

People eat lots of extras with fish and chips such as mushy peas, pickles, pickled onions, gravy, and even curry sauce.

Pickled onions

Fish and chips

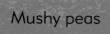
Mushy peas

A pickle

In the UK, it's also traditional to eat fish and chips at the seaside, or shore. At the end of a day on the beach, families eat an outdoor supper of fish and chips before heading home.

Fasting for Ramadan

For Muslims, Ramadan is the holiest month of the year. During this time, adults and teenagers fast, or don't eat, between sunrise and sunset.

Children sometimes fast for just half the day.

Each evening, after sunset, families and friends gather for a special evening meal called *iftar*.

Many people break, or stop, their fast each evening by eating fruit called dates.

A family eating iftar in Indonesia

An iftar meal in the United Arab Emirates

Ramadan is when God, or Allah, first revealed parts of Islam's holy book, the Quran (kuh-RAN). During Ramadan, Muslims say extra prayers, fast, and try to give up bad habits. Fasting is a way to show their faith in Allah. It also helps people remember that not everyone has enough to eat.

No Food to Eat

Not everyone around the world has enough to eat.

Many people are too poor to buy food.

Many people live in places where they cannot grow food.

Every night, millions of adults and children go to bed hungry.

These people are looking for food in a garbage dump.

In Brazil's cities, many children live on the streets. They have no parents or grown-ups to take care of them. They sleep in cardboard boxes and search for food in garbage bins. **Charities** and other helpers try to bring food and drink to the street children.

Street children in Brazil eating food from charity workers

Where in the World?

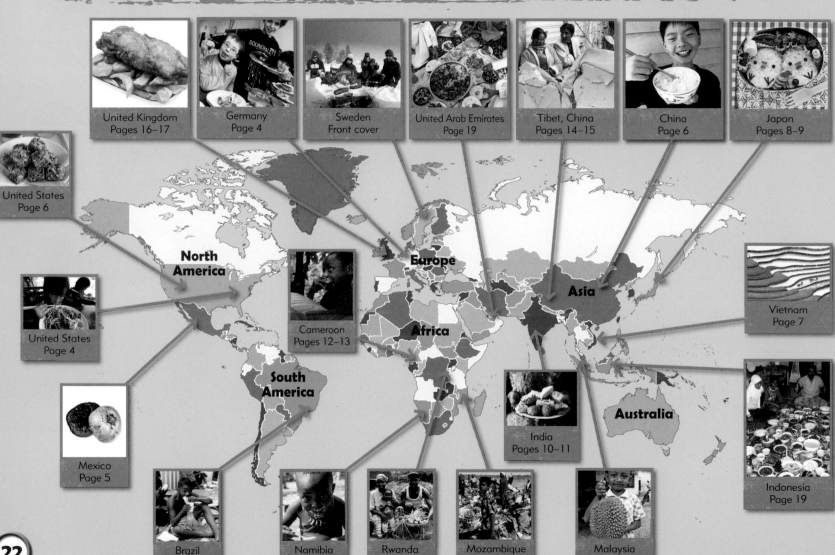

United Kingdom
Pages 16–17

Germany
Page 4

Sweden
Front cover

United Arab Emirates
Page 19

Tibet, China
Pages 14–15

China
Page 6

Japan
Pages 8–9

United States
Page 6

United States
Page 4

Mexico
Page 5

North
America

Europe

Asia

Africa

South
America

Australia

Cameroon
Pages 12–13

Vietnam
Page 7

India
Pages 10–11

Indonesia
Page 19

Brazil
Page 21

Namibia
Page 4

Rwanda
Page 5

Mozambique
Page 20

Malaysia
Page 5

Glossary

charity (CHAR-uh-tee)
An organization that raises money and uses it to do good work such as helping people living in poverty.

festival (FES-ti-vuhl)
A day or several days when a large number of people enjoy a celebration. Most festivals are connected to special times in a religion.

hunter-gatherer (HUHN-tur GATH-ur-ur)
A person who gets most of his or her food by hunting, fishing, or gathering wild foods.

ingredient (in–GREE-dee-uhnt)
A food or substance that is used to make a particular dish or meal. For example, flour, eggs, and sugar are the main ingredients used to make a cake.

pickled (PIK-uhld)
Put into vinegar or salty water. Foods such as onions and mini cucumbers are often pickled. This gives them a tangy taste and makes them last for a long time.

plow (PLOW)
To dig up the soil with a large tool that is called a plow. Soil is plowed to make it soft and crumbly and ready for young plants or seeds to be planted. A plow can be pulled over the ground by an animal or a tractor.

rain forest (RAYN FOR-ist)
A thick forest of trees and other plants. More than 13 feet (4 m) of rain falls in a rain forest each year.

spices (SPEYE-siz)
Dried parts of plants, such as seeds, that are used as ingredients in cooking. Spices are used to give foods more flavor or different colors.

traditional (truh-DI-shuh-nuhl)
Something that has been done in a certain way for many years by a group of people. For example, eating a particular type of food.

Index

Read More

Beer, Julie. *Weird but True Food: 300 Bite-size Facts About Incredible Edibles.* Washington, DC: National Geographic (2015).

Falk, Laine. *This Is the Way We Eat Our Food (Scholastic News Nonfiction Readers).* New York: Children's Press (2009).

Learn More Online

To learn more about food around the world, go to
www.rubytuesdaybooks.com/food